FUNHOUSE

Also by Efrayim Levenson

For My Relations
Buffalo, NY: Poetrymanz Press, 2000

Dances with Tears
Hoboken, NJ: Poets Wear Prada, 2007

Jewish America: A Brief History of a One-Sided Love Affair
Kindle Editions, 2010

FUNHOUSE

Poems by

Efrayim Levenson

POETS WEAR PRADA • Hoboken, New Jersey

Funhouse

Copyright © 2013 Efrayim Levenson

All rights reserved. Except for use in any review or for educational purposes, the reproduction or utilization of this work in whole or in part in any form by electronic, mechanical or other means, now known or hereafter invented, including xerography, photocopying and recording, or in any informational or retrieval system, is forbidden without the written permission of the publisher.

> Poets Wear Prada
> 533 Bloomfield Street
> 2nd Floor
> Hoboken, NJ 07030
> http://pwpbooks.blogspot.com/

First North American Publication 2013
First Mass Market Paperback Edition 2013

Grateful acknowledgment is made to *Parkside Poets Collection 2012* and *River Poets Journal* where some of these poems previously appeared.

ISBN-13: 978-0615848853
ISBN-10: 0615848850

Printed in the U.S.A.

Front cover photo: Levenson Family Archives
Author photo: Craig Fishbane

Dedicated to the blessed memory of

Brant Lyon,

a true poetry warrior for our time

Table of Contents

Foreword

Acknowledgments

Tickets, please! / 1

Day One
    Sea Lion / 5
    Fragile Strings / 6
    Tearburst / 8
    A Warm Chord / 9
    Beyond Any Ink / 10

Day Two
    Miles of Thoughts / 13
    Soft Head / 14
    Headache / 15
    In a Baked Dream / 16
    Modesty Rant / 17
    Merry-Go-Round / 18

Day Three
    Lead Bucket / 21
    Under an Iron Sky / 22
    Grasshopper / 23
    Angels / 24
    Tomorrow / 25

… Aren't you glad …

About the Author

Foreword

I am writing this from the perspective of a musician that has worked with a lot of great poets. I like Efrayim's work because much of it is informed by his humanity, music, his relationship to specific artists and a multitude of other sources. The expression of his musical relationship somehow translates his experience into words on a page that evoke a mood very similar to how listening to music can make one feel. Imagine a lone guitar riff playing behind "Beyond Any Ink" ... soulful, bluesy, and a little quirky; a surrealistic merry-go-round sound behind "Merry-Go-Round"; or some Miles Davis gently behind "Miles of Thoughts."

Another important element in music is silence. Good use of silence can have a drastic impact on the listener's emotional response and also stimulate the imagination. In contrast to more musically oriented pieces, Efrayim makes good use of silence in his work. I can imagine solo voice for pieces like "Under an Iron Sky" or "Angels." To me, those pieces stand out because the subject matter is very compelling and one's imagination could suffice.

One element that makes all forms of art great is the ability to inspire imagination. It is only when you notice that you have been absorbed by a work, or re-visit it many times, that you know you have in some way connected with the spirit of the artist. Moreover, great art connects us to our human past, as it is our oldest form of intellectual and spiritual expression, telling us the stories of the range of human experiences over long periods of time. Whether you find music in Efrayim's work or not, I hope you will agree that his work does inspire the imagination and adds many pages to the book of humanity.

Clif Jackson

Acknowledgments

This chapbook is a collection of poetic interpretations of the music of Buckethead. CDs listened to over the course of its composition are:

Giant Robot, Sony Japan/CyberOctave/Higher Octave, 1994
Death Cube K, *Disembodied*, Ion Records, 1997
Colma, Higher Octave, 1998
Monsters and Robots, CyberOctave/Higher Octave Music, 1999
Cobra Strike, *The 13th Scroll*, Ion Records, 1999
Cobra Strike II: Y, X+B, X+Y, Ion Records, 2000
Electric Tears, Meta, 2002
Kaleidoscalp, Tzadik, 2005
Enter the Chicken, Serjical Strike, 2005
Cornbugs, *Rest Home for Robots*, TDRS Music, 2005
Deli Creeps, *Dawn of the Deli Creeps*, TDRS Music, 2005
With Travis Dickerson, *Chicken Noodles*, TDRS Music, 2006
Gorgone, TDRS Music, 2007
STILL Shine, *Lightyears*, Ion Records, 2007
From the Coop, Avabella, 2008
Death Cube K, *Torn from Black Space*, Rare Noise Records, 2010

"Fragile Strings," "Miles of Thoughts," "Lead Bucket," and "Sea Lion" originally appeared in *Parkside Poets Collection 2012*. "Miles of Thoughts" was also published in *River Poets Journal*.

Thank you very, very much for your invaluable contributions: Blanche Mackey-Williams, Clif Jackson, Dave Schmeidler, Devorah Levenson, Downtown Music Gallery, Marissa Levenson, Parkside Poetry Workshop, Roxanne Hoffman, Jack Cooper, Steve Dalachinsky, and Tom Galley.

Tickets, please! You're the next victim — I mean, *customer* — in my funhouse. Step right up! Get your life distorted! For just two tickets! See the three-headed cashier, on your way in. (Don't you just *love* the smell of his smile?) Bruisings and beatings, at every turn! It's a bumpy ride on this odyssey through my mind! Are you strapped in? Better get that seat belt on, and your shoulder harness, too!

Tickets, please! Hundreds of fleas a-buzzing in my parietal lobe know *which* limb to sever, in this happy tale of woe … Can't see them? Well, they can see you — and they want to eat your carcass. Not much fun for you, *eh*? My frontal lobe hosts robot pawns indentured in a game of chess. Watch them fight over just how to wipe the asses of queens and kings: royal pains who wriggle out of their own rules! It's an uphill battle — just for you! One never paid — in full — until you're dead! My cerebellum is a hammer aimed at your skull. You'll squirm so *beautifully* as your life oozes away — so little time for memories.

Look out!

Ah, just missed …

DAY ONE

SEA LION

Hope remains on the faces
of this morning's new recruits

Soon they will live and die
simultaneously
in this merciless place

They may not eat tomorrow
asleep in cold loneliness
roving in wood-paneled basements
from one end of town to the other

Their savior
has not been seen
or heard
since the first was cast away

The rails' rumble carries robots
who bite hallucinations
as they collide with shadows
and one another

How many have missed their stops
holes chewed in their brains
at the sight of beached sea lions
dry humping subway-platform floors?

FRAGILE STRINGS

I

The key to my life opens the wrong door
reveals quiet pain, lonely surrender.
No intention is a fortune
that weighs too much.
No one else will carry it for me.

I bend, I break, I flatten out
become pavement
for progeny to roll over
a distant memory
for a *gone world*.

Love is a sieve that bleeds
becomes tainted in bright darkness.
It doesn't matter how many times
repeated, this process —
a cruel place to deliver a message.

Here disease grows without food or water.
I wasn't sent with a cure.

II

The key to your life was here
only for a visit
to tug you away with fragile strings.
Found is lost in front of your eyes.

You bend, you break, you flatten out
become a puddle, undifferentiated in rain.
Truth is too big
for hope to hold
in this porous vessel.
Tears wait for the burst to call.

TEARBURST

Hope for peace
quiet in the distance
too small on the horizon
to see just yet
beyond life's relentless storm
that weakens your defenses
until you become a mirage and

cry to relieve pain
cry to lose weight
cry to immerse in purity
cry to unfreeze stunned numbness

Your tears sing to all of us
not a note out of tune
Then you open your mouth
drink replenishing rain and

breathe

A WARM CHORD

Who will reach for tomorrow
on whom brightness of eyes shine
what loss prevented in the day's promise?

There's a warm chord to strum
in every discord, cherished music
in every wrong move

Oh, to rescue each of six strings
to set free an a cappella breeze
in any of six directions

Tomorrow, the dizziness precedes the swing
of the piñata-stick through the whirlwind
that closes in on a drizzle of fingers

Tomorrow, the song that carries us to the doorway

Oh, to be a helping hand in these times
of pain multiplication, to serenade
the rock, the roll, the stroll
through the too well known

Oh, to hope, to hope, to hope in a downpour

BEYOND ANY INK

Through windows of the train ride
along twilight's edge we saw angels
torn from parachutes, canned
in their own juices.

The monster's pursuit is relentless
his roar miles ahead, far beyond
any ink to paint. The Earth shudders
with each stomp as fire flies
from his robot eyes.

We won't eat much, just sit
in our quiet corners, hidden in headphones
filled with guitar-strum shreds.

You can water us like plants or pets,
a little herb maybe to keep us calm,
a few psalms for our souls.
We need all the strength we can get.

DAY TWO

MILES OF THOUGHTS

Sunrise looms for an unlikely day
that ends in sunset tones of crickets and cicadas
in a language few understand
a soundscape for a vision quest

Only a heartbeat is heard in the stillness
as a million miles of thoughts race
to the front of the line to make
your breath-quickening acquaintance

Sing to me no words
dance on a drummer's sticks
heal me with six strings again
weave me into a pullover poem with full orchestration

SOFT HEAD

A one-of-a-kind spider named
Babba-ba-babba-cha-cha-cha
bites into the fog
to pierce the soft thoughts
of my routine day

Not a muscle dares twitch
breathless I stare
trapped in its web
as it serenades me:

Gun to your head
Gun to your head
You're better off read
than heard

Your future is bright
on this conflicted night
nailed-down tight
without a word

Reality shoots down dreams
with laser beams
that hear the screams
of birds

A smoking puddle
of nearsighted mumblings
emerges and crashes
here
crashes
there
crashes

HEADACHE

For the crime of filling my eyes
with shredded medicine
I am marched to the guillotine,
ready to begin my popcorn-puppet dance.
Led, victorious, by cheers,
screams of dizzy laughter from the jesters
who are sure being poor is only a fashion statement.

The world will be a better place without you as one of its remnants!

Has life ever seemed an endless game of rummy?
I can't remember the taste of Tanqueray
but I know the smell of the lime.

Demands pile up, means dwindle;
I daydream on the platform.
Crowds of lovers and haters gather
for the performance of a time
more opportune to put a check in the mail.

Before the master craftsman
can position me, I know it's too late:
even roars will not drown out
the sound of a blade descending.

I'd have a headache if I still had a head.

IN A BAKED DREAM

A dream bounces into view
of mannequins singing in a crooked dollhouse —
a new language only the walls understand.

It's rhythmic chalkboard-scratch chatter
to me a prop of pretzel dough
waiting to be baked. Their leader, in pre-coffee

blindness, stomps in, stumbles on his plastic friends,
manipulates me for the oven. I awake, braided,
covered with egg yolk, in a pitch-black room.

The temperature: 350 degrees.

MODESTY RANT

It's only April and cleavage season has already started! Aren't you bored by it? Wouldn't you like something different? Don't you want to see a woman with three tits? Don't you want to see a woman with eleven tits? Each tit monogrammed with the name of a player on the 1969-Super-Bowl-losing Minnesota Vikings? What'd you say? 1970? Who cares! Don't you want to see throbbing pussies on the backs of double-jointed knees that don't know which way to run?

Don't you want to see?
I want to see.

Don't you want to see?
I want to see.

Don't you want to see?
I want to see.

Don't you want to see?
I want to seeeeeeeeeeee a woman, beautiful in her modesty, long skirt and long sleeves, covered-hair she shares only with her husband, Shabbos candles dancing in her eyes, a royal daughter of G-d.

MERRY-GO-ROUND

The merry-go-round of torment
shoots sparks as it whirls through the darkness.
An ominous dawn approaches with a knock
that drowns the door in frantic water.

Is anyone home?

We yearn for cries of crows
that march in controlled impatience
screams of strings
to bounce in electric exhaustion.

We run for cover from the static laughter
of desert thunder on our search
for true peace in the quiet.

An end always begins.

DAY THREE

LEAD BUCKET

Did I make it home okay yesterday? I'm still in a ditch on the parkway, screaming in Braille at the light show that in seconds stopped traffic for miles ... Yeah, like those gawks on the other side are going to help any! Hey, I'm over here! Can't you see my yarmulke floating in the sludge? Next time, I won't stop for you, either ... I'm the only one who knows how to drive anyway and I have an expired license to prove it. So hoist me out of here! I have a freight train to catch to my Midtown job — one game of inches and seconds, exchanged for another ... Don't you worry that pretty little bucket-of-lead head of yours. I'll be back, to torment your asphalt cracks into submission — until you beg me to stay home. You'll beg me. I know you will.

UNDER AN IRON SKY

Under an iron sky, water recedes from the heat
while we sing to our babies gurgling
in air-conditioned ease
a sweet lullaby of comfortable urban life

What amount of love will change
the fate of the world outside
as drought closes in
on our islands of joy?

Can't we hear the beat
of its march to our doors?

Soon our music will be reduced
to wordless cries
untranslatable in the heat of day and night

Still we recite *Songs of Ascents*
to keep the groundwater down

GRASSHOPPER

In this familiar place I'd never forget
warmth glows from the hearth.
Your flamenco hair swishes
and sways to the sound of that heat,
but I never remember your name.

Birds' songs soothe; ducks
call; grasshoppers accompany
your guitar's cry to dance —
crickets play their song of night.

Sleep well, tomorrow's
a new creation.
There's much work ahead
in this game of inches and seconds.

Are you still equipped?
There's no choice, only place to rest,
some time to slow your mind.
Close your eyes, hush your sighs,
another day rises soon.

Anticipations echo.

ANGELS

Choral night
Thunder approaches
Schematic gusts play chimes
A siren sings

Angels of the pitch-black night
signal each other in whispers
Rhythmic punches reach for me
piercing slaps *Ahhh!*
I wince again and again and again

A solemn guitar tries to soothe
accompanied by faint
chirps of birds,
crickets,
water drops

Out of bewildered breath
I fail to escape
Ahhh! I am pulled north to south
Uhhh! stretched east to west
eyes so wide search the deceiving stillness

Again! *Ohhh!*
I retch and writhe
in their punishment

Another alarm calls for the end
of my sentence
Night sounds now heal,
calm in a lullaby of bells that drifts me
to sleep, sleep, sleep ...

TOMORROW

A fog of clarity brings tomorrow
reflects your heart, your breath
smiles with you, cries —

sometimes out of tune
Tomorrow, a canopy of torrential rain
or the deepest blue

a forest of concrete or the darkest green
Tomorrow, a song of rhythmic alarm
or the call of the whippoorwill

... Aren't you glad you came to my funhouse? I know you enjoyed it. Visit me next time you're in town. I should have the table saw fixed by then. Be careful going home. There's a full moon tonight. I can already hear the howls.

About the Author

Efrayim Levenson began writing poetry in 1982, in Buffalo, New York. His work has since appeared in numerous online and print publications, among them: *River Poets Journal, Parkside Poets Collection, What Happens Next?, ArtVoice, Poetica, Medicinal Purposes,* and Chabad of Rego Park's *Poetry Corner.* A former executive director of Niagara Erie Writers, Efrayim has collected his poems in two previous chapbooks: *For My Relations* (Poetrymanz, 2000) and *Dances with Tears* (Poets Wear Prada, 2007). "& Ribbon," from the latter, received nomination for a 2008 Pushcart Prize.

Levenson's collaborations with musicians, such as Clif Jackson (Secret Orchestra), Dave Schmeidler (Skyrats), and Rey Scott (Sun Ra Arkestra) led him, initially, to poetic interpretation of instrumental music. *Funhouse* is his latest endeavor.

He lives in Far Rockaway with his daughter, Marissa.

www.ingramcontent.com/pod-product-compliance
Lightning Source LLC
Chambersburg PA
CBHW061518040426
42450CB00008B/1673